Václav Havel was born in Czechoslovakia in 1936.
Among his plays, those best known in the West are
The Garden Party, *The Memorandum*, *Largo Desolato*,
Temptation, and three one-act plays, *Audience*, *Private
View* and *Protest*. He is a founding spokesman of
Charter 77 and the author of many influential essays
on the nature of totalitarianism and dissent. In 1979 he
was sentenced to four and a half years in prison for his
involvement in the human rights movement. Out of this
imprisonment came his book of letters to his wife, *Letters
to Olga* (1981). In November 1989 he helped to found
the Civic Forum, the first legal opposition movement in
Czechoslovakia in forty years; in December 1989 he was
elected President of Czechoslovakia; and in 1994 became
the first President of the independent Czech Republic.
His memoir, *To the Castle and Back*, was published in
2007. *Leaving* is the first play written by Václav Havel
since he was propelled to political office in 1989.

Paul Wilson lived in Czechoslovakia from 1967 to 1977,
when he was a member of the rock band the Plastic People
of the Universe. Since his return to Canada in 1978 he has
translated more than twenty books of Czech literature into
English, including several other of Havel's plays, notably
The Memo (a new translation of *The Memorandum*),
Guardian Angel and *The Beggar's Opera*, and prose work
including *Open Letters*, *Letters to Olga*, *Disturbing the
Peace*, *Summer Meditations*, *The Art of the Impossible*
and his recent memoir, *To the Castle and Back*. He works
from Toronto as a freelance writer and editor.

VÁCLAV HAVEL

Leaving

translated from the Czech
by Paul Wilson

European Book Club
Czech Center
N.Y. September 30, 2010

ff

faber and faber

First published in 2008
by Faber and Faber Limited
3 Queen Square, London WC1N 3AU

Typeset by Country Setting, Kingsdown, Kent CT14 8ES
Printed in England by CPI Bookmarque, Croydon, Surrey

Odcházeni © Václav Havel, 2007
This translation © Paul Wilson, 2008

The right of Václav Havel to be identified as author of
this work has been asserted in accordance with Section 77
of the Copyright, Designs and Patents Act 1988

A CIP record for this book is available from the British Library

ISBN 978–0–571–24709–7

2 4 6 8 10 9 7 5 3 1

Author's Note

If this play is to resonate properly, it must be acted in a civil manner: seriously, soberly, normally. It should not be tarted up with grotesque movements, clever staging ideas, exaggerated gestures or intonations, mugging, biomechanics or anything striking that attempts either to explain, interpret or illustrate the text, or simply to make it more amusing. The author also suggests that not a lot of cuts be made to the text, especially not random cuts. He has come to this conclusion not out of a blind attachment to his own words, but from practical experience: cuts can easily tear the web of meaning that holds the play together, or can disrupt the play's own rhythm, usually resulting – paradoxically – in greater boredom than might be the case if the text were left as it is.

Translator's Acknowledgements

I would like to thank:

Sam Walters and his actors for their dramatic reading
of an earlier draft of the play at the Orange Tree Theatre
last year, and for their suggestions during rehearsals
this August; Tom Stoppard for generously reading my
translation and making many helpful suggestions,
particularly in places where I was still clinging too tightly
to the original; Marketa Goetz-Stankiewicz for, among
other things, pointing out connections with Havel's
earlier work that enhanced my understanding of the play;
Jitka Sloupová, Havel's agent and a translator in her own
right, for catching some inconsistencies in my translation;
Jan Zelenka, Havel's Czech editor, for many helpful
clarifications; Martin Vidlák, Havel's assistant, for
facilitating communications with the author; Václav
Havel, for taking time to talk to me about how he saw
the characters and the story.

And a special thanks to my partner, Patricia Grant, for
her fine ear for dialogue and for her love and assistance
at every stage of this project.

Leaving had its first English production at the Orange Tree Theatre, Richmond, on 19 September 2008. The cast, in order of appearance, was as follows:

Zuzana Fay Castelow
Dr Vilem Rieger Geoffrey Beevers
Irena Carolyn Backhouse
Monika Paula Stockbridge
Grandma Auriol Smith
Oswald James Greene
Victor David Antrobus
Hanuš Stuart Fox
Dick Mike Sengelow
Bob Paul O'Mahony
Vlasta Esther Ruth Elliot
Albín Christopher Naylor
Knobloch Philip Anthony
Bea Weissenmütelhofová Rebecca Pownall
Patrick Klein Robert Austin
Constables Paul O'Mahony, Mike Sengelow
The Voice The Voice of the Author

Director Sam Walters
Designer Sam Dowson
Lighting Designer John Harris
Stage Manager Stuart Burgess

Notes

Most of the characters' names can be pronounced as they would be in English. There are, however, one or two exceptions. Albín should be prounounced AHL-bean; Hanuš as HA-noosh; and the character referred to by Rieger on page 25, Dobeš, as DOE-besh. The stress is always on the first syllable.

Quotations from *The Cherry Orchard* by Anton Chekhov are taken from Michael Henry Heim's translation in *Chekhov: The Essential Plays* (New York: Modern Library, 2003). Quotations from Shakespeare's *King Lear* are taken from the Kittredge edition, although those familiar with Shakespeare may notice that some of the lines, mostly in Act IV, are not precisely as they appear in Shakespeare's text. I felt I had the licence to deviate slightly since, in the original play, Havel takes those lines from a new Czech translation of *Lear* by Martin Hilsky, who is outstanding for his renditions of Shakespeare into modern, idiomatic Czech.

P.W.

Characters

Dr Vilem Rieger
a former Chancellor

Irena
his long-time companion

Grandma
his mother

Vlasta
his elder daughter

Zuzana
his younger daughter

Monika
a friend of Irena

Bea Weissenmütelhofová
a political scientist
and multicultural sociopsychologist

Albín
Vlasta's husband

Hanuš
a former secretary to Rieger

Victor
a former secretary to Hanuš

Oswald
a servant in the Rieger household

Dick
a journalist

Bob
a photographer

Patrick Klein
a deputy, and later the Vice-Prime Minister

Knobloch
a gardener

First Constable

Second Constable

The Voice

The play is set in the orchard of the Rieger villa

LEAVING

Act One

The orchard outside the Rieger villa. Upstage steps lead to the entrance to the villa, on one side of the stage. On the other side, opposite, is a coach house, and centre upstage a gazebo. Centre downstage is a set of garden furniture, a table with some chairs around it. A swing hangs from the branch of a tree. Rieger's daughter, Zuzana, is alone on stage. She is sitting on the swing, which is swaying gently back and forth; she has a large set of earphones on her lap, along with an open laptop on which she is writing something with both hands. She has a mobile phone clamped between her shoulder and ear.

Zuzana (*speaking into the phone*) Yeah . . . Aha . . . Okay . . . Marvellous . . . Brilliant . . . Me too . . . Very much. No, you're the one, Lili . . . Okay, talk to you soon . . . Bye.

Zuzana turns the phone off, slips it into her pocket, puts the earphones on and continues working on the laptop, oblivious to her surroundings. A short pause, then Rieger strolls slowly onto the stage. He's a greying, elegant man of about sixty in a navy-blue blazer and a cravat. Irena, his companion, about forty, enters with him, along with Monika, Irena's self-effacing friend, and Grandma, Rieger's mother. There is a somewhat regal, ceremonial air about their entrances. Rieger, who is clearly the focus of attention, sits down, while the women gather around him. A short pause.

Irena Are you warm enough?

Rieger Yes.

Irena You can't possibly be warm enough!

Rieger I assure you, darling, I am quite warm enough.

Irena Let me bring you a blanket.

Rieger I don't need a blanket. I don't want a blanket. I am quite comfortable as I am.

Grandma Let him be. Stop treating him like a child.

Irena Monika, would you please? The brown one. It's right there in the hall, on the armchair.

Monika You mean the beige one?

Irena Yes.

Rieger Monika, please. I'm perfectly fine.

Monika, at Irena's silent command, exits into the villa, passing Oswald on the steps. He's a general factotum in the household. He is carrying a glass with a hot toddy in it on a tray, along with a napkin and a spoon. He stands in the background, ready to serve.

Grandma There are several beige blankets in there, and they're in a bit of a mess, they haven't been to the cleaners in donkey's years, and anyway, they're not very warm.

Rieger What's keeping those reporters? Weren't they meant to be here by now?

Victor, Rieger's former secretary, enters from the coach house.

Victor I simply don't understand it, sir. People can't just come and go as they please when you're visiting the Chancellor! I've called them and apparently they're on their way.

Irena Vilem, you have to tell them exactly what you think. None of your diplomatic pussyfooting around. People would be very disappointed in you –

Victor Precisely. You have to be firm.

Grandma Vilem doesn't need to be told what he should do. He's always had a way with reporters.

Victor exits into the coach house. Monika enters from the villa with a beige blanket. She hands it to Irena, who drapes it around Rieger's shoulders.

Rieger I think it's time for my afternoon toddy.

Oswald steps up to the table, lays out the napkin and the spoon, and then sets down the drink.

Thank you, Oswald. How did you sleep?

Oswald Very well, thank you, Mr Chancellor.

Irena *(to Oswald)* It's time to peel the potatoes for dinner. When you've put them on to boil, empty the washing machine and hang everything out to dry on the line over there among the cherry trees. The clothes pegs are in their usual place under the sink, and be careful not to spill the rubbish when you're getting them. You might take the rubbish out while you're at it – but not until you've finished hanging out the laundry. And don't forget to put in a new bin-liner.

Zuzana's mobile phone starts to play the 'Ode to Joy'. She works a little longer at her laptop, then closes it, removes her earphones, takes her mobile phone out of her pocket and puts it between her ear and shoulders, leaving both her hands free. She slides off the swing, takes the computer and earphones, and walks towards the villa.

5

Zuzana (*speaking into the phone*) n't have to, really . . .
Right . . . Yes . . . Right . . . No, there's nothing to worry
about! . . . Exactly! . . . Exactly! . . . No, absolutely not!
. . . Great! . . . Great! . . . Brilliant! . . . Okay, talk to you
soon. Bye.

Zuzana exits into the villa.

Irena (*to Oswald*) Don't even think about just emptying
the rubbish and putting the old liner back in the bin. It
makes an awful smell. Monika will be along shortly to
make sure you've done it properly, and generally give
you help and advice. Won't you, Monika?

*Monika nods. Oswald bows and exits, with the tray,
into the villa. He passes Hanuš, Rieger's former
secretary, on the steps. Hanuš is carrying a huge,
garishly painted portrait of Rieger.*

Hanuš (*to Rieger*) Good news, Vilem. You can keep this.
The chancellery stamp on the back is so smudged that if
it comes down to it, we can always say we simply didn't
notice.

Rieger Let them have it. It's a shoddy piece of work
anyway.

Grandma I want it. I'll hang it in my bedroom.

Rieger Mother, please. We're not going to clutter the
house up with fourth-rate finger paintings.

Irena We'll keep it. But it doesn't belong in Grandma's
room. She can put up some of your childhood pictures
if she wants. It's going in my room. Besides, it's not half
bad, is it, Monika?

*Monika shrugs her shoulders. A short pause. Hanuš
looks questioningly at those present, and then takes
the portrait back into the villa. Victor enters from the
coach house.*

6

Victor They're here!

Grandma Who's here? The reporters? How many of them are there? Wouldn't it be better if they stayed on the other side of the fence?

Irena Monika, would you be kind enough to take Grandma inside? She can watch television, or read yesterday's *Keyhole*.

> *Monika ushers Grandma into the villa. On the steps they pass Oswald, who enters carrying a tray with three glasses of beer. He stands respectfully in the background. Victor comes out to meet Dick, a reporter, carrying a bag over his shoulder, and Bob, a photographer, with several cameras slung round his neck.*

Victor Mr Chancellor, this is Dick. He's a well-known reporter, and this is Bob, who's going to take a few pictures, if that's all right with you.

Rieger May I ask which paper you work for?

Dick Various foreign journals, all world-class papers, I hasten to add. And some domestic ones as well.

Rieger Which domestic ones?

Dick Well, for instance, I work for *The Keyhole*. I interviewed you fifteen years ago, in Athens, do you remember?

Rieger I've given so many interviews.

Dick It was right below the Acropolis.

Rieger I was there with Papandreou, wasn't I?

Dick Exactly.

Rieger Very well, please take a seat.

Dick sits down at the table, and takes a sheaf of notes, a notebook, and two recording devices from his bag. Victor stands a little way off. Bob walks around, looking for interesting shots and taking pictures with different cameras. Dick shuffles through his notes until he finds what he is looking for.

Dick (*reads*) Can you tell us, Mr Chancellor, how, after so many years spent in –

Irena Would you mind introducing us?

Rieger Yes of course, sorry. This is Irena, my long-time companion.

Dick Dick.

Irena It's an honour to meet you, Dick.

Dick (*to Rieger*) Your long-time companion is utterly charming.

Rieger Thank you.

Dick (*reading*) Can you tell us, Mr Chancellor, how, after so many years spent in –

Irena Excuse me, but is there anything I can get you?

Dick That's kind of you, but I'm fine. Or – come to think of it, a couple of beers would hit the spot. For Bob and me.

Rieger I'll join you.

Dick Do you think I could have a bit of cinnamon with that?

Oswald steps forward with the tray and puts three glasses of beer on the table, pulls a small packet out of his pocket, and shakes some cinnamon into Dick's beer.

Irena (*to Oswald*) Did you find the clothes pegs?

Oswald I haven't looked yet.

Irena Well, when you do, be careful not to knock over the bin. And could you send Monika out?

Oswald bows and exits, with the tray, into the villa.

Dick (*reading*) Can you tell us, Mr Chancellor –

Rieger I'm not the Chancellor any more –

Dick Can you tell us, Mr Former Chancellor, after so many years spent in high office, how you feel in the role of an ordinary citizen again?

Rieger I feel quite comfortable about it, mainly because I now have far more time to spend with my family. On the other hand, it's only now that I realise how deeply people believe in the traditions, values and ideals that I've come to embody in their eyes, and which, now that I've left office, appear to be losing ground with each passing day –

Monika enters from the villa. Irena removes the blanket from Rieger's shoulders and hands it to Monika.

Irena Would you be kind enough and bring me my compact – the new one; my hairbrush – the old one; and my lipstick – the dark one. They're either in the left-hand shelf in my bathroom, or on my night table, or on the first shelf from the top in the right-hand cupboard in the hall – or wherever.

Monika Wouldn't you like me to bring you your dark glasses and that silk wrap you bought at the Midget Brothers'?

Irena What a lovely idea! Yes, please do.

Monika exits into the villa.

I'm sorry, but I didn't know you were going to be taking pictures as well.

Dick (*reading*) Which of the values you fought for, Mr Former Chancellor, do you consider the most important?

Rieger At the very core of my political thinking there was always the individual human being – a free, happy citizen, constantly learning new skills and steeped in family values –

Irena Dick, don't you love the way he can put things in a nutshell? I've always admired that.

Victor The Chancellor speaks beautifully and expresses himself very clearly. I hope you'll put it all down exactly as he said it.

Rieger The government exists to serve the citizen; the citizen does not exist to serve the government.

Victor I'd quote that word for word!

Rieger I've always wanted our country to be safe and secure. And not just our country. The whole world. And safe and secure not just for humanity, but for all of nature. (*He declaims.*) Not, however, at the expense of economic growth!

The Voice I would remind the actors to play their parts as civilly and naturally as possible, with no grotesque or comic overacting. They should not try to make the play more entertaining by using exaggerated facial gestures. Thank you.

> *Hanuš enters from the villa, carrying a telephone in each hand.*

Rieger This is Hanuš, my former secretary. He's helping me sort out a few things. (*To Hanuš.*) I hope *they're* not government property.

Hanuš Unfortunately, Vilem, they are.

Hanuš walks across the stage with the telephones and exits into the coach house. Monika enters from the villa with the hairbrush, the lipstick and the compact, dark glasses and a silk wrap. She gives everything to Irena, who immediately starts putting on her make-up. Hanuš enters from the coach house, walks across the stage, and exits into the villa. Dick leafs through his notes. After some time, he finds the next question.

Dick (*reading*) Mr Former Chancellor, how did you turn the ideals you stood for into public policy?

Rieger Well, for instance, I placed great importance on human rights. In the name of freedom of expression, I imposed significant limits on censorship. I honoured the right of assembly, and during my terms as Chancellor, fewer than half of all public demonstrations were broken up by the police. And I respected freedom of association. Just witness the dozens of citizens' groups that arose spontaneously from the grass roots –

Irena Excuse me, Vilem, but you really should mention that you respected the opinions of minorities as well.

Rieger And I respected the opinions of minorities and in some cases I had absolutely no hesitation in sitting down with various independent or single-issue groups.

Victor In that regard, the Chancellor was truly broadminded. Often to a fault. You should have seen the kind of riff-raff that turned up sometimes!

Oswald enters from the villa with a bag of rubbish and a tray on which there are three glasses, a small amount of beer in each one. He puts down the bag and respectfully stands in the background.

Irena I think he did a lot for women, too.

Rieger I have always had great regard for women and I've always surrounded myself with them.

Dick Great headline!

Victor (*to Dick*) That's something we might discuss later.

Rieger I waged a merciless war on bribery and corruption. Everyone remembers the Klein affair, surely. Would you like a little more beer?

Dick Well, but really, just a little.

Oswald approaches with the tray, puts the beer on the table, takes a package of cinnamon out of his breast pocket and sprinkles some into Dick's beer. He bows, and heads toward the villa with the tray, just as Grandma is entering.

The Voice This business with the cinnamon: there is no psychological or any other explanation for it whatsoever. Or at least as far as I know there isn't. For now, let's just call it a product of pure authorial whimsy, or of my somewhat self-centred delight that I can come up with any hare-brained idea at all and the actors will have to play it with a straight face. But what can I do? The simple fact is, I like it and I feel it belongs there.

Oswald exits into the villa. On the steps he passes Grandma, who enters with a copy of The Keyhole *in her hands. Irena finishes applying her make-up, then puts on her dark glasses, takes them off again, plays with her wrap and subtly strikes a number of poses while Bob dances around her, taking pictures.*

Grandma Let him be now! You can see how tired he is.

Rieger I'm not tired, Mother.

Grandma Yes, you are. I can hear it in your voice. Anyway, you always say the same thing every time.

Irena That's not true! He spoke beautifully today.

Victor I agree. It turned out exceptionally well today. But, as the saying goes, best to stop while you're ahead. One more question, please.

Rieger Do you know what Tony Blair once told me? If you don't answer their questions, they'll answer them for you. That's good, isn't it?

Dick Right, then, one more question. Does the loss of parliamentary immunity bother you?

Rieger Why should it bother me?

Dick And aren't you worried that –

Victor I'm sorry, but really –

Dick And aren't you worried, Mr Former Chancellor, that –

Victor I'm sorry, but we really must wrap it up now.

Dick Aren't you worried, Mr Former Chancellor, that you'll be forced to move out of here? This villa, after all, is government property.

Rieger, Irena, Monika, Grandma and Victor all look at each other in surprise. A pause.

Rieger They wouldn't dare.

Dick makes a few more notes, then puts his notebook and his recording devices into his bag, gets up and shakes hands with Irena and Rieger. Bob takes some final pictures.

Dick If we have any follow-up questions, may we come again?

Irena Of course you may, Dick.

Dick and Bob make to exit, accompanied by Victor.

Victor I'm sure you'll understand if we ask to take a look at your piece before you publish it. Just a quick once-over, and we'll return it to you straight away. Could you do that for us?

Irena (*calls out*) We'll choose the pictures together, won't we, Dick?

Dick and Bob exit. Victor returns.

Victor Mr Chancellor, my congratulations! You were magnificent!

Rieger The most important thing is to know how to call things by their proper names, to address the big picture, put things in their proper context. A good leader, of course, will surround himself with a good network of think-tanks.

Victor I'm sorry, what did you just say?

Rieger A network of think-tanks. Did you notice that they completely forgot to ask about the economy or social policies? Or about education, for that matter. I deliberately mentioned Klein, who was made deputy yesterday, and I expected them to latch on to that and ask me more about it – but they didn't. Odd, isn't it?

Victor It's sad, Mr Chancellor, the sort of people you have to give the time of day to. I'm going to carry on.

Rieger Can't you just lay off for now?

Victor We can't let that bureaucrat Hanuš do all the work!

Victor exits into the coach house. Vlasta enters with her husband, Albín. She is Rieger's elder daughter. She holds a basket of fruit, Albín is carrying some official folders.

Vlasta Hello, Father; hi, Grandma; hello, Irena; hi, Monika. I'm bringing you some fruit. Help me, Albín –

Vlasta and Albín put a variety of fruit on the table.

Irena (*calling out*) Oswald!

Grandma Vlasta, did you know what a reporter said here just now? He said we might have to move out. Where would we go, for heaven's sake?

Irena Monika, would you mind looking to see what's become of Oswald? When you find him, tell him, please, to bring me three baskets with napkins and several fruit knives, and some watered-down beer for Albín, and then to keep an eye on those potatoes. When they're ready, he should drain them nicely, then let them dry and cool down, and then peel them. But he shouldn't use a regular potato-peeler! He just has to remove the skin with a little knife.

Monika Does he know which one?

Irena He can use any knife he wants as long as it's not the fancy one Mrs Putin gave us.

Monika exits into the villa.

Vlasta People are talking a lot about your moving out. They say you don't need fancy government digs any more. If the worst comes to the worst, you – I mean you, Grandma and Zuzana – can move in with us. You know how much we love you, don't you, and how grateful we are to you for everything?

Rieger And what about Irena?

Irena No need to worry about us. Monika and I will find something, a sublet somewhere. The main thing is that we should be nearby.

Rieger That's so kind of you, Irena.

Hanuš comes out of the villa with a huge bust of Gandhi in his arms. He stands in front of Rieger.

Hanuš I'm sorry to say we can't keep this. Fifteen years ago, someone included it in the office inventory.

Rieger To hell with them!

Hanuš I almost hesitate to bring this up, Vilem, but a set of rulers is missing as well. Do you know anything about it?

Rieger No, I don't!

Victor enters running from the coach house.

Victor (*sharply*) They were all given out as souvenirs. There's none left, and you shouldn't be bothering the Chancellor with this at all!

Hanuš exits into the coach house with the bust in his arms. Victor follows him. At the same time Monika enters from the villa, carrying a tray with a basket, some little knives, napkins and a glass of watered-down beer.

Irena Well?

Monika He's probably gone to sleep somewhere.

Monika sets everything down on the table and puts the fruit into the basket. Albín takes the watered-down beer. A pause.

Rieger It was a gift from Indira.

Grandma (*to Vlasta*) Are you staying for dinner? We're having new potatoes with cheese and butter.

Knobloch, the gardener, enters, carrying a rake.

Vlasta Shall we stay, Albín?

Albín shrugs his shoulders.

We'll just have a bite and then be on our way.

The Voice I know that nothing much has happened so far, but I wanted the play to start very slowly. That way, the audience will be all the more grateful when the pace gradually begins to pick up.

Hanuš enters from the coach house, walks across the stage, and exits into the villa.

Rieger How do you do, Mr Knobloch? So, are we going to have a good crop of cherries this year?

Knobloch A bumper crop, if you ask me.

Rieger And what's new out there in the big wide world? What do people think about things? Have you seen any demonstrations supporting me? Or any posters, at least?

Knobloch The lads in the pub are talking about the move.

Rieger What move?

Knobloch Deputy Klein says the government simply can't afford to be handing out villas to every Tom, Dick and Harry.

Victor rushes in from the coach house.

Victor It's just been on the radio!

Rieger What?

Victor Deputy Klein announced in a media scrum outside parliament that the government simply can't afford to be handing out villas to every Tom, Dick and Harry.

A wind rises, and it starts to rain.

End of Act One.

Act Two

The orchard outside the Rieger villa, one hour later.
Everything is as it was at the end of Act One. The wind
and the rain have died down. The stage is empty. After
a few moments, Vlasta and Albín, who is carrying files,
Rieger and Irena, followed by Monika and Grandma,
enter from the villa, one after the other.

Rieger Will you stay with us a while longer?

Vlasta Fine, but just for a while.

Grandma Why were the large potatoes not properly
cooked, and the small ones overcooked?

Irena (*to Monika*) Could you please tidy away all this
make-up?

Monika starts putting the items of make-up on a tray.

Vlasta (*to Rieger*) Father . . .

Rieger Yes?

Vlasta We – that is, Albín and I – would like to discuss
something with you.

Rieger Go ahead.

Irena Grandma, it's time you were going inside. There's
a cold damp coming off the ground. Monika, could you
please –

Monika takes the tray with the make-up, the wrap
and the dark glasses, then takes Grandma by the hand
and exits into the villa with her.

Vlasta Father, you know how much Albín and I love you. We only want what's best for you. It's a bit awkward, but it's what everyone does, because you never know what might happen. And so we thought – that is, Albín and I thought – that we should – as a family, I mean – be ready for anything.

Rieger Are you referring to the possibility that sooner or later, we might have to move out of here?

Vlasta I've already made myself clear about that: you would come and stay with us – at least for the first few days, until you found something else. But there are many other things to consider as well.

Rieger Such as?

Vlasta Oh, I don't know. The furniture, the pictures, the books, the bank accounts, living expenses. The long and short of it is, Albín and I have already talked to a friend of ours, a lawyer, and tried to come up with a proposal.

Vlasta takes the file from Albín. Monika enters from the villa.

Rieger You mean a will?

Vlasta It sounds awful, doesn't it? But what I mean by that is a certain set of instructions in case there are any doubts about what belongs to whom.

Irena You mean when Vilem dies?

Vlasta No need to jump straight to the worst conclusion. We all want Father to live as long as possible. For that reason, our proposal takes different alternatives into account. It might seem terribly formal, of course – in this family, everything has always belonged to everyone – more or less – but given the times we live in, anything might happen. For instance, they could easily enact legislation to legalise the seizure of private property in cases where there is justified suspicion of evading an investigation into suspect activity.

Rieger In other words, you want me to transfer my property to my nearest and dearest.

Vlasta To the members of your family –

Rieger What about Irena?

Irena Don't worry about me – Monika and I have plenty tucked away, don't we?

Monika nods.

Rieger That's so kind of you, Irena.

Irena (*calls out*) Oswald!

Vlasta You should look this over, think about it, and perhaps discuss it with someone. Albín and I don't want to rush you, we only think it would be pointless and silly to let ourselves get caught out just because we weren't thinking ahead. All we have to do is come up with an arrangement that won't tangle us up in a lot of red tape, and won't land us on the front pages.

Irena Vlasta's right, Vilem. You know the kind of thing *The Keyhole* can get up to. (*To Monika.*) Shall we go?

Monika nods, and Irena and Monika exit. Vlasta hands the file to Rieger, who puts it aside on the table. Vlasta, then Albín, embrace Rieger and exit. Knobloch approaches with a rake in his hands.

Knobloch So, you're expecting a visitor?

Rieger Me? No –

Knobloch Deputy Klein said on television that he plans to pay you a visit soon.

Rieger He said that?

Knobloch exits. Shortly afterwards Bea appears with a book in her hand. For a moment she simply stands and looks at Rieger, who finally becomes aware of her presence.

Are you looking for anyone in particular?

Bea You.

Rieger And how can I help you?

Bea Would you be willing to sign my copy of this book of your speeches?

Rieger Of course.

Rieger motions Bea to come closer and sit down, and she does so, somewhat hesitantly. Rieger also sits down and takes out a pen. Bea opens the book to the title-page and sets it in front of Rieger.

Now, don't tell me you've read the whole thing.

Bea Actually, I've read it rather carefully, first because I found it absolutely fascinating, but also because I wrote my doctoral thesis about you. It was my own idea. My thesis is called: 'Vilem Rieger's Conception of Democracy'.

Rieger And how did it turn out?

Bea Excellently. I've been interested in your ideas for years. I probably know more about you than you do yourself. And the longer I study you, the greater the impact your work has on me.

Rieger So, you're a political scientist?

Bea Yes, but I've taken a couple of terms of multicultural sociopsychology and intermedia communications.

Rieger May I ask what your name is?

Bea Weissenmütelhofová . Beatrice Weissenmütelhofová
. But you can call me Bea, Mr Chancellor.

Rieger Delighted, Bea. But I'm no longer Chancellor.

Bea For me, you will always be Chancellor, Mr
Chancellor.

*A pause. Rieger takes one of the baskets of fruit from
the table and offers it to Bea.*

No, thank you. I didn't come here to eat your food, or
even take up much of your time.

Rieger You're not eating my food, or taking up my time.
Go ahead – have one.

Bea Thank you, I will.

*Bea chooses an apple and eagerly takes a bite. Grandma
quietly enters from the villa. Rieger and Bea don't see
her. There is a longish pause as Bea eats her apple.*

Is this from your orchard?

Rieger No, my daughter brought them. This is just a
cherry orchard.

Bea Once, in Charkov, you spoke very movingly about
your orchard. You said it was the symbol of our cultural
tradition, of how we shape the landscape in our own
image.

Rieger Ah – that was so long ago. Do you mind my
asking which of my speeches, or ideas, most caught your
fancy?

Bea As I understand it, Mr Chancellor, the basis and the
main source of your politics is the idea that the individual
must be at the very core of that politics, and that everything

we do in politics should be aimed at helping him, or her, develop themselves in the broadest possible way. But the idea that our country ought to be safe and secure was also important. And how right you are about that! How could anyone develop themselves in the broadest possible way in a place that was unsafe or insecure? I also love the idea that you put forward fifteen years ago, in Taiwan: the notion that human beings are made for freedom.

Rieger Ah, yes, I remember that speech made quite an impression at the time. Chiang Kai-shek even asked me for my original copy.

Grandma I certainly hope you didn't give it to him.

Rieger and Bea turn to Grandma in astonishment.

Rieger Mother, this is Bea – Bea, this is my mother. Bea wrote her thesis about me –

Grandma How lovely. Should I go looking for Oswald?

Rieger Just make sure he didn't leave something burning on the stove.

Grandma goes back into the villa. A pause.

Bea I'd love to write your life story sometime. You must have experienced so many fascinating things!

Rieger Yes, I've lived through quite a lot and I've accomplished a great deal. There's so much that only a few people know about, or that no one knows about at all.

Irena and Monika enter. They are carrying paper and plastic bags with the shopping. When they see Rieger and Bea, they stop.

Irena I see we have a visitor.

Rieger This is Beatrice Weissenmütelhofová, a political scientist and multicultural sociopsychologist who has also studied intermedia communications. She's a student of my politics and she's going to write my biography. This is Irena, my long-time companion, and this is Monika, Irena's friend.

The women shake hands.

Irena I bought you a cap.

Monika takes a sporty peaked cap with 'I Love You' written on it and hands it to Irena, who puts it on Rieger's head.

Rieger Thank you, darling.

Monika picks up all the bags and exits with them into the villa.

Irena You have a very pretty admirer. But then, you always did. And you always managed to find time for them. It's interesting, men don't seem to write about you.

Rieger There's Dobeš –

Irena The one who writes for *The Keyhole*? That's hardly something to brag about. Anyway – please don't let me interrupt you.

Irena exits into the villa.

Bea I don't think your long-time companion was too pleased to see me here.

Rieger She's very much in love with me, which means that she can sometimes be a problem. I'd be delighted to tell you about my life. I have a lot of time on my hands these days, and I'm rapidly forgetting things, so the sooner we begin, the better.

Bea Could I come tomorrow, early evening? I'm really looking forward to working with you. Well – goodbye.

Rieger Goodbye, Bea.

Rieger hesitates a moment, then quickly kisses Bea on the cheek. She strokes his hair, then picks up her book and runs off. Klein slowly, somewhat ceremoniously approaches, accompanied by Knobloch, with his rake, and Victor. Rieger quickly stuffs the hat into his pocket.

Knobloch You have a visitor, Mr Chancellor.

Rieger Patrick Klein. What a surprise! Please, sit down. Can I get you something?

Klein Some tea, perhaps –

Rieger Victor, would you do the honours?

Victor bows and goes into the villa. Knobloch exits as well.

Klein So – how's life? I suppose you have more time for your family now. Or do you miss politics?

Rieger It's something of a paradox, but it's only now that I realise how many supporters I really have. It seems I must, after all, have embodied some values that people hold dear.

Irena enters from the villa.

Irena Hi!

Klein Hello.

Rieger We were just saying that I have a lot of supporters.

Irena Yes, many people have expressed their interest and their fellow feeling. Hardly a day goes by without some journalists dropping in, or young students planning to write something about him.

Rieger Irena's not exaggerating. But, as Havel once told me, popularity isn't everything.

Victor enters from the villa with a cup of tea, followed by Monika. Victor gives the tea to Klein.

Victor Can I get you anything else?

Klein No, thank you. Unless there's a tiny drop of rum to go with it.

Irena The rum is just inside the door, on the left, above my hats and below where Vilem keeps his shoes.

Victor nods and exits into the villa.

Klein Clever young man.

Rieger That's Victor, the former secretary of my former secretary Hanuš. He's helping us separate our private things from those that belong to the Chancellor's office. You wouldn't believe how difficult that is. But of course, you'll go through the same thing one day.

Rieger laughs long and hard at his own joke.

And what about you? How are you enjoying your new position?

Klein You know how it is; so far, I'm just trying to work out who's with us, and who is merely pretending to be with us.

Victor comes out of the villa with a bottle of rum. He goes up to Klein and puts a few drops of rum into his tea.

Thank you, Victor. Do you mind if I ask you for one more tiny little thing? I do love biscuits with my tea.

Irena They're on the table, Monika. Unless Oswald has squirrelled them away somewhere. He has his own little system of hiding places. Not long ago, for instance, I discovered that he'd put a box with five kinds of cheese in it behind the refrigerator. Imagine that – five kinds of cheese! God knows how long they'd been there, so of course I threw them out.

Monika exits into the villa. Victor stands back.

Rieger I hear you're about to become a cabinet minister.

Klein The boss told me that at this point in time, he can't imagine anyone better for the post, and he's prepared to put my name forward, so the matter's on the table, but it's not yet top of the agenda.

Rieger Victor, you can go home now. You can carry on in the morning.

Victor With your permission, I'd like to finish sorting through one more important box.

Rieger What's in it?

Victor Some of your private correspondence.

Rieger You can burn it.

Irena No, put it aside, and I'll go through it later.

Rieger (*shouts*) Burn it!

Klein Your archives shouldn't really be destroyed. One day they'll have immeasurable value. At the very least, young Miss Gambacci, at the Intergovernmental Historical Commission, should take a look at them.

Victor Rest assured, Mr Klein.

Victor exits into the coach house. Monika enters from the villa with a plate of biscuits. She puts it down in

front of Klein, who immediately starts to eat them,
and will continue to eat them until his exit.

Klein Thank you, Miss.

Monika Monika.

Klein Thank you, Monika. You are very kind and you have such a nice name. I've always had a soft spot for Monikas.

Irena She's my friend. Monika, would you please try to wake up Oswald?

Monika If I can find him.

Monika exits into the villa.

Klein May I speak freely in front of Irena?

Rieger Certainly.

Klein The reason I came –

Rieger I'm listening –

Klein It would be unfortunate for you and your family, and an embarrassment to the new leadership, if you suddenly had to move out of here, given that you've made such a contribution to the country, and everyone knows how you've made this place your home over all those years, and how fond of it you are, and that you really have nowhere else to go.

Rieger I appreciate your seeing it that way, Patrick. To tell you the truth, I'd never given it much thought. I suppose I just took it for granted that we'd be able to stay on.

Klein As did I! I didn't really pay any attention to the matter until my advisors pointed out that someone could start digging into this – and you can just imagine what a field day a rag like *The Keyhole* would have with that.

Rieger What do you suggest?

Klein That the government rent it out to you. Naturally, for an affordable sum – that's something we could easily defend.

Rieger That wouldn't be so bad. What do you think, Irena?

Irena As the Queen of Sweden once said to me, nothing is free.

Klein I haven't come here to offer some kind of deal, certainly not where one's hearth and home is concerned. I have to say that any such interpretation would be a personal insult, not only to me, but to the entire leadership. That is really and truly not how we wish to do politics, and anyone who thinks we do would be making a terrible mistake, one that we could simply not let pass without some kind of response.

Rieger Easy now, Patrick. Irena didn't mean it that way.

Victor enters from the coach house carrying a stuffed briefcase.

Victor Goodbye.

Klein Look after yourself, Victor. I'm sure we haven't seen the last of each other.

Victor We certainly haven't, Mr Deputy.

Victor exits.

Klein On the other hand, it has to be said that the new leadership, Vilem, does not wish to see you as an adversary and it certainly has no intention of bringing anything to a head. What good would that serve? It could only lead to instability. So it's only logical that part of the agreement would be that you too – at least in public – would not come out against us in any way.

Rieger But Patrick, you surely can't expect me to say things – about certain people – that I don't really believe?

Klein We couldn't care less what you think about us.

Irena So what's your point?

Klein (*to Rieger*) It would be in the interests of political harmony in the country if, at the appropriate time and in the appropriate place and in the appropriate way, you were to let it be known that you support the new leadership because you do not wish to question the democratic system in this country and the legal instruments that are now in place. After all, we too wish to put the individual at the centre of our political agenda, and we too want our country to be a safe and secure place.

The Voice I have the feeling that this dialogue, as important as it is to the play, might also be somewhat boring. But it's not entirely my fault. Of course, I have an influence on my own play, undeniably, but the main thing is that, when I write, I try to serve the logic of the thing itself, which seems more important to me than my own feelings. For better or worse, I am merely mediating something that transcends me. I can't rule out one other possibility: that I'm just making excuses for myself. How easy it is, after all, to blame everything on 'something beyond ourselves'. Sometimes, when I see everything that gets blamed on 'something beyond ourselves', I feel sincere regret.

The actors all look at Rieger. A short pause.

Rieger I'll give it some thought.

Klein Vilem – you know I've always had the highest regard for you. That's why I'm asking you to stand with both feet planted firmly on the ground. If I don't get a positive answer from you by tomorrow, I'll know what that means.

Klein gets up, takes one more biscuit from the plate, and calls out to Irena.

My best to Monika!

Klein exits.

Irena Vilem?

Rieger Yes, darling?

Irena What was in that private correspondence?

Rieger I really couldn't say.

Irena Something intimate?

Rieger You know very well I've always chucked things of a sensitive nature into the fire.

Irena Into the fire? Your pants are on fire, you liar! (*She calls out in different directions.*) Oswald! Oswald! Get up!

End of Act Two.

Act Three

The orchard outside the Rieger villa. A day later. Oswald is alone on stage, rearranging the garden furniture. Irena enters, accompanied by Monika and Grandma. Irena sits down, the other women gather around her.

Irena Where's Vilem?

Oswald The Chancellor is taking a bath.

Grandma Now? In the afternoon?

Oswald He'll be out soon. I heard the water running out of the tub ten minutes ago, and he's probably now shaving, applying aftershave, gelling and combing his hair. Then all he'll have to do is get dressed.

Irena Aha, he's got an interview. Monika, would you mind?

Monika The maroon sweater?

Irena If it's not wrinkled.

Monika I'll check.

Irena Thanks.

Monika exits into the villa.

Oswald, could you please dig out that hand-painted plate we got from the Ceausescus, put the fruit Vlasta and Albín brought yesterday on it, get some napkins, small plates and knives and bring it all out here.

Grandma Are you expecting those reporters again? I wouldn't bother telling them anything more. Vilem's told them everything.

Oswald bows, and exits into the villa. He passes Hanuš, who is coming down the steps.

Hanuš Is Vilem not here?

Irena As you can see.

Hanuš I wanted to ask him about something. Just some final details about office supplies.

Irena Don't tell a soul, but he was really sorry to have to give up the Gandhi.

Hanuš So was I.

Hanuš exits into the villa, passing Monika on the steps. She's bringing make-up, the maroon sweater and dark glasses. She puts everything on the table. Then Irena gets up, strips down to her brassiere and puts the sweater on. She hands her discarded top to Monika, sits down again, and starts putting on her make-up and combing her hair. Monika exits into the villa with the clothing.

The Voice It happens all the time: I remember something I'd forgotten, but then immediately afterwards, I forget what it is I've just remembered. It's getting serious. I'm always forgetting who's on stage, who's just exited, what mood they were in when they left the stage, and so on and so forth. I might easily have someone make an entrance and then never have them leave the stage. Or, on the contrary, they might exit at the beginning, then never return. Or I might require them to enter when they're already on stage, or exit twice in a row without

having entered in between. I think I'll write poetry
instead.

> *Monika exits into the villa. A few moments later
> Rieger enters from the villa. He is nattily dressed and
> groomed, and he's visibly applied pancake make-up.
> His hair has been dyed a dark brown.*

Irena (*still putting on make-up*) They're blackmailing
you.

Rieger I know.

Irena You should never have told them you'd think it
over.

Rieger It's just a turn of phrase.

Irena If you endorse them, you'd be spitting in your own
face. I couldn't respect you any more.

Rieger I know.

> *Oswald enters from the villa with a tray, carrying
> a large hand-painted plate with fruit, along with
> napkins, small plates, little knives, and a bottle of
> champagne and flutes. He puts the fruit and the other
> things on the table and retreats to the background,
> where he stands, waiting to be of service. Victor enters
> from the coach house.*

Victor They're on their way. Could I mention one small
thing?

Rieger Did you burn it?

Victor I think, Dr Rieger, that you should be firm, but at
the same time diplomatic. If you are too dismissive of the
new leadership too soon, it could be counter-productive,
because it could seem that you simply haven't been able
to accept it – that you are still harbouring a grudge, or

nursing some bitterness, or a sense of betrayal, or a feeling that you are irreplaceable, or something like that.

Irena Some advisor you have!

Rieger Victor's not my advisor; he's the former secretary of my former secretary, Hanuš. Did you burn it?

Victor I'm sorry, but I had to tell you what I think, forgive me. When they get here, I'll bring them in.

Rieger Did you burn it or didn't you?

Victor Time! Time! There's never enough time!

Victor exits rapidly into the coach house. Irena finishes putting on her make-up and brushing her hair; she puts away her make-up and puts the dark glasses up on her head.

Rieger Mother, would you look to see if any of our cherries are ready to pick?

Grandma If you'd like.

Grandma exits into the villa. She passes Monika on the steps.

Irena You were strutting about like a peacock in front of that Weissenmütelhofová person yesterday, wasn't he, Monika?

Monika shrugs her shoulders.

It was ghastly to watch. I was utterly ashamed of you. Do you think you have to demean yourself in front of every piece of skirt that happens along? Monika, surely you agree –

Monika shrugs her shoulders.

Rieger That's all nonsense. I behaved with that young lady the same way I'd behave with anyone else.

Irena Listen to him. A lady? Sssss –

Offstage, the 'Ode to Joy' sounds, then suddenly stops. Zuzana enters from the villa, carrying an open laptop and earphones with a mobile phone clamped between her ear and shoulder. She heads for the swing.

Zuzana (*into the phone*) Now? All right, why not, Lili? Yes . . . Yes . . . I can do that. Fine. Brilliant! See you soon . . . Bye.

Zuzana puts the mobile phone in her pocket, sits down on the swing, opens the laptop, puts on the earphones and starts working on the computer. She pays no attention to anything going on around her. A pause.

Irena Do you love me?

Rieger Yes.

Irena More than you love this house?

Rieger Yes.

Irena More than the orchard?

Rieger Yes.

Irena More than politics?

Rieger Yes.

Irena More than you love yourself?

Rieger Yes.

Irena I think you're talking complete rubbish.

Victor enters from the coach house and goes to meet Dick and Bob, who are approaching. Grandma enters from the villa carrying a basket. She walks across the stage and exits.

The Voice What I love about the theatre are the entrances and the exits and the re-entrances, entering from the wings and onto the stage. It's like going from one world into another. And on stage, I love gates, fences, walls, windows, and, of course, doors. They are the frontiers between different worlds, cross-sections through space and time that carry information about their contours, their beginnings and their ends. Every wall and every door tells us that there is something on the other side of it, and thus they remind us that beyond every 'other side' there is yet another 'other side' beyond that. Indirectly, they ask what lies beyond the final 'beyond', which in fact opens the theme of the mystery of the universe and of Being itself. At least that's what I think.

Dick sits down, opens his bag and takes out his notes, a notebook, and two recording devices. He places everything in front of him, then takes out several copies of The Keyhole, *shows them to everyone present and then puts them on the table as well.*

Dick Tomorrow's *Keyhole*. For you.

Irena Thanks, Dick. Don't you have today's?

Dick You haven't seen it?

Irena We only have yesterday's.

Everyone except Zuzana takes a copy; some remain on the table. Irena and Monika leaf through their copies for a while and then put them down. Victor, who is standing a little way off, is holding his copy in his hands. Bob walks around the stage, taking pictures, trying to get shots of people holding The Keyhole.

Rieger I have an idea, my friends. This is my first major interview after these huge changes in my life, and I enjoy working with you. Let's have a glass of champagne to celebrate!

Everyone nods. Oswald immediately passes around the flutes, opens the bottle, and pours it. He removes a small packet of cinnamon from his pocket and starts to put a little in Dick's champagne.

Dick No, thanks – not today.

Bob I'll have some, thank you.

Oswald sprinkles some cinnamon into Bob's glass. There is a general toast.

Rieger So – here's to our health. May everything turn out well for every one of us. It may be that difficult times lie ahead. But if we stick together, if we can all just like each other, even just a little, if we listen to each other and try to understand each other, they can't touch us.

Irena We're with you, Vilem. Please, be with us.

Dick shuffles through his notes until he finds the question he was looking for. He turns on the recording devices. As Rieger responds, he writes down the answers in his notebook.

Dick (*reading*) Dr Rieger, could you tell us what the essence of your economic policies were when you were Chancellor?

Rieger That's a good question. The essence of my policy was an effort to significantly reduce the burden on taxpayers. All taxes were gradually reduced, some were eliminated altogether, such as the tax on the interest on inherited interest. Lowering taxes was meant to stimulate economic growth, which in turn would enable the government to gradually increase pensions and social security payments, so that everyone would really benefit. Is that clear enough?

Irena Shouldn't you mention your favourite slogan: 'Less government'?

Rieger Ah yes, less government, lower taxes and higher pensions and benefits. That's it in a nutshell.

Dick (*reading*) And how did your policies impact on women?

Rieger Going forward, we intended to bring in a special bonus for working women who also had a home and a family to look after.

Irena You talked a lot about that. You called it 'dish money'. We used to make fun of it. Remember, Monika?

Monika smiles and nods.

Victor Sorry to butt in, but it might be appropriate to point out that these were policies with a very long time frame.

Rieger Of course, it couldn't all have been accomplished right away. But on the other hand, we wanted to put an end to the politics of procrastination.

Dick As far as economic policy is concerned, I'd like to just ask – (*He quickly shuffles through his notes.*) – how you intended . . . what you intended – (*He finds the question.*) – what you intended to do to attract foreign investment?

Rieger We had several instruments for achieving that. Are you drinking? Does everyone have enough? Oswald, could you top people up?

Oswald pours everyone more champagne. Hanuš enters from the villa.

Hanuš Vilem –

Rieger For instance, when a potential foreign investor wanted to build something – a warehouse, let's say – we would have cut down the trees, cleared the undergrowth, levelled the ground, brought in water, sewage, gas, electricity, internet access, and built roads and parking lots. At the same time, this would increase employment, which would in turn decrease unemployment.

Hanuš Vilem –

Rieger On the other hand, we wanted to provide incentives, including zero-sum or negative-sum tax payments, and special profit-based rewards –

Hanuš Vilem –

Rieger And then, thirdly we – what was the third thing, Victor?

Victor I can't remember, Dr Rieger.

Hanuš Vilem, please –

Rieger Wasn't it an offer to fund a polyfunctional promotional campaign for qualifying corporations?

Victor I don't know. Yes. Maybe. Perhaps.

Irena nods to Monika, who approaches Irena, who then whispers into her ear while Monika nods.

Hanuš Vilem – I'm sorry to interrupt, but we have a minor problem.

Rieger What is it?

Hanuš Several days ago, according to the administration department records, you took out a hundred erasers, fifty coloured pens, a litre of ink, and ten packages of paper. Shouldn't we be returning some of that, at least?

Victor (*shouts*) Don't bring that up, Hanuš!

Hanuš But we don't want to leave ourselves open to attack over such trivial items.

Rieger Don't be such a nervous Nellie!

Irena has finished whispering to Monika, who exits into the coach house. Hanuš exits into the villa. Dick, after searching for a while, finds another question.

Dick (*reading*) How would you respond, Dr Rieger, to critics who accuse you of not waging a tougher war on bribery and corruption, especially among our leading politicians?

Rieger The exact opposite is true. It was I, after all, who first drew the public's attention to some rather shady transactions involving Klein.

Irena When a politician buys five luxury homes, all at the same time, for himself and his extended family, doesn't that strike you as a little odd? Vilem talked about this openly and what happened? Everyone attacked him for it, and Klein just laughed. Isn't that so, Vilem?

Rieger It is.

Victor To be precise, we did not press charges, so in the formal sense –

Rieger Charges or not, everyone knows that with just a little more time, I would have given bribery and corruption a good run for its money. After all, it's been a priority of mine for the last fifteen years.

Monika enters from the coach house, goes over to Oswald and whispers something to him. He nods, then bows and exits into the coach house. Monika gestures to Irena that something has been settled.

If I might venture beyond the bounds of your question: I have always believed that decency and morality were

42

extremely important in the marketplace. I simply wanted this country to be a safe place. For everyone.

Irena You've already said that, Vilem.

Rieger Some things bear constant repetition. For instance, the idea that there are times when freedom must be defended by force. After all, that's why we have an army, a police force, an intelligence service, a counter-intelligence service, a second police force, a militia, special forces, first-strike commandos, an army – and so on.

> *Grandma enters with a basket full of cherries. She's accompanied by Knobloch, who is carrying a rake. Oswald enters from the coach house with another bottle of champagne. He opens it and tops up everyone's glasses, while quietly laughing to himself.*

Irena I brought this champagne back fifteen years ago from Paris. We bought it on the Boulevard St Germain with Jack Lang. He loved this champagne, especially the 1915 – October *cru*. (*To Oswald.*) What are you laughing at?

Oswald Yepichodov broke a billiard cue.

Irena What's Yepichodov doing here? And who let him play billiards? I don't understand these people!

> *Oswald suppresses a laugh, then quickly clears the unnecessary things off the table, the empty bottles etc., puts them on a tray, bows and exits into the villa. Grandma shows everyone the cherries.*

Grandma There's going to be a bumper crop this year. What will we do with all those cherries?

Knobloch When I was young, those cherries would be dried, pickled, marinated and made into jam. They were so soft and sweet and juicy, those dried cherries. They smelled so good.

43

Rieger You're not the only one who remembers that, Mr Knobloch. I'd rather hear what's new. What are people saying about me? Do they feel the same vast intellectual and spiritual abyss between me and the current leadership as I do? The thing is, these journalists here are going to write about it.

Knobloch People *like* Vice-Prime Minister Klein.

Rieger What? He's Vice-Prime Minister already?

Knobloch I heard it on the radio just a while ago. (*He points to* The Keyhole.) May I?

Rieger Go ahead.

> *Knobloch takes a copy of* The Keyhole *and exits. Grandma also takes a copy and makes to exit into the villa with her basket of cherries, looking at the paper as she leaves. Dick leafs through his notes and finally finds a new question. Grandma pauses before exiting into the villa.*

Grandma Angelina had breakfast with Brad in an Indian restaurant.

> *Grandma exits into the villa.*

Dick (*reading*) And now to change the subject a little – do you still feel young, or do you feel you've aged?

Rieger Haven't aged a bit, mentally or physically.

Dick (*reading*) How does your long-time companion, Irena, get along with your mother and daughters?

Rieger Irena gets along well with almost everyone. (*Calls out.*) Mother!

> *Grandma appears in the doorway of the villa, holding* The Keyhole.

Tell the gentleman how well you get along with Irena.

Grandma Just fine.

Dick (*reading*) Do you think, Mrs Riegerova, that your son and his long-time companion Irena are fond of each other?

Grandma Vilem's rather afraid of her.

Irena He's not afraid of me in the slightest, and he tries to get his own way. But I respect that and I always try to accommodate him, because I have enormous regard for him. And I love him.

Dick And do you also love your long-time companion Irena?

Rieger Yes. Could I say something?

Irena There are some things he's terribly shy about and it's impossible to get a sensible word out of him –

Rieger Could I say something?

Irena – yet in other things he's not shy at all.

Dick What kind of things?

Rieger Could I say something about my education policies?

Dick Go ahead.

Victor We didn't really accomplish a great deal in that regard.

Rieger I wouldn't say we were complete failures either. I wanted those who went through our school system to come out as wise, decent, and well-rounded, well-educated people. That was the main idea behind my plan for school reform. If it was slow to be realised, that was mainly the fault of some teachers who were not themselves sufficiently wise, decent or well-educated.

Dick Have you been faithful to Irena, your long-time companion?

Rieger (*insulted*) Of course I have!

Dick When did you last have sex?

Rieger (*angrily*) That's none of your damn business!

Dick But it would certainly interest readers of *The Keyhole*.

Rieger (*shouting*) Fuck them!

The Voice I would urge the actors to act naturally, not to raise their voices pointlessly, to avoid pathos, to articulate their lines well, to stick to the text, and not resort to histrionics. Thank you.

> *Dick turns off the recording devices and puts everything back in his bag.*

Dick I think that's everything. May I?

> *Dick positions himself between Rieger and Irena, putting his arms around their waists. Bob takes their picture from all angles.*

Can we take a few more shots inside?

Irena But please, be quick about it.

> *Irena exits into the villa, followed by Dick, Bob, Victor and Monika. Rieger exits last, but he stops on the steps. Zuzana also stops.*

The Voice When a playwright requires a character to be alone on stage, or have a conversation the others are not meant to hear, he usually tries to devise ways to usher the unnecessary characters off the stage. Shakespeare didn't worry about such things. His characters simply walk on or walk off as he required. Today, there are many complicated ways of getting actors offstage. Often, they leave to prepare something to eat. That's also a way of ensuring that when it's time for them to come back, their entrance will be natural because, in the meantime, they will have got something ready, and they can bring it onstage at the right moment. I wonder if having the characters go into the villa collectively for a photo shoot will seem too arbitrary a way of getting them out of the way so that something can happen that they are not meant to witness? Yes, I admit, I need them off the stage. I would add, however, that it is customary for newspapers to run photographs of the subject of a major interview at home, and for members of the family to be present, if only to do a quick tidy up or make sure the journalists don't steal anything.

Zuzana continues working on her computer. Rieger notices that Bea is now on stage.

Rieger Bea –

Bea Is it true they're trying to evict you?

Rieger They'll rent this place to me if I support them publicly. They said they would continue with my policies.

Bea That's rubbish. They may say they are guided by your political principles, but it won't be genuine, because all they're interested in is power. You've been strong all your life – that's who you are, that's your identity – and after all you've gone through, you can't just give up. We're all going to try to find you a suitable place to live.

Rieger That's so kind of you, Bea.

Bea kisses Rieger.

Bea You smell so nice.

Rieger It's partly for you.

Bea You seem far younger than you do on television. You have hardly any grey hair.

Rieger You have no idea how badly I sometimes need encouragement. And kind words from a young, pretty, wise, well-educated creature make me feel twice the man.

Rieger and Bea look at each other intensely for a moment, and Rieger suddenly embraces Bea and begins kissing her. Bea gently struggles, more for show, to get out of his embrace.

Bea No – not here!

Rieger Come!

Rieger takes Bea by the hand and leads her quickly into the gazebo. They embrace and kiss. Oswald enters from the villa running. He is laughing, and in each hand he holds half of the broken billiard cue. He examines the break, shaking his head, laughing. Then he exits into the coach house. The 'Ode to Joy' sounds from one of Zuzana's pockets. She puts the computer aside, walks downstage, takes out the mobile phone and turns it on. The 'Ode' stops. Zuzana listens intently. For a moment, there is utter silence.

Zuzana (*into the telephone*) And your point is?

At that moment, the wind rises and it begins to rain.

End of Act Three.

Interval.

Act Four

The orchard outside the Rieger villa. The same day, a short while later. The wind and the rain have died down. Rieger and Bea are hugging and kissing in the gazebo. Oswald is sleeping in the bushes not far away, but he can't be seen.

Irena (*calls from offstage*) Vilem! Darling! Where are you?

Irena enters, followed by Monika. She stops close to the gazebo, then something catches her attention, and she looks inside and sees Rieger with Bea.

Vilem!

Rieger and Bea quickly emerge from the gazebo, and rearrange themselves in great embarrassment. Irena glares at Rieger for a moment, and then slaps his face.

Rieger Ow!

A short pause, then Irena slaps Rieger in the face again.

Ow!

A short pause, then Irena starts quickly slapping his face over and over, while Rieger tries to fend off the blows.

Rieger Ow – I'm sorry – I can explain . . . Ow!

Irena What's there to explain? You're a ridiculous, selfish, miserable, dirty old man. Or more precisely, you're the parody of a dirty old man.

Bea Goodbye!

Bea exits, Rieger comes up to Irena and tries to caress her. She pushes him away.

Irena Why do you think I had the French champagne brought out? Because today is our fifteenth anniversary! I deliberately waited to see if you'd remember it. Naturally, you forgot. And not only that, you betray me on this very day, and in the very gazebo where we had such wonderful, wild times together.

Rieger You're making too much of this. She merely kissed me – I couldn't very well push her away, could I?

Monika leans toward Irena and whispers something to her. Irena nods and then yells in different directions.

Irena Oswald! Oswald! The onions are burning.

Oswald gets up, looks around sleepily, bows, and goes into the villa.

Have you ever thought how much I've given up because of you? My flat. My place as a make-up artist with the Midget Brothers. Family. My flat. My cottage. My friends. My flat. My best friend –

Rieger Best friend?

Irena You've never met him . . . My flat. I lived only for you and through you. I did everything to satisfy your needs, to make your life easy and harmonious. I accepted a role as your shadow and enhanced your career in so many ways. I patiently endured everything around you – including your mother. You say the individual is at the heart of your politics, but you haven't a clue what love is. You're just as cynical as all the rest of them.

Rieger Who do you mean by 'all the rest of them'?

Irena All of you lot. Monika, we're leaving.

Irena takes Monika by the hand and exits with her.
Rieger goes to follow her.

Rieger (*calling out*) Irena! My dearest! Forgive me! It was just a silly little thing.

Vlasta enters with Albín.

The Voice I don't know what it is exactly, but something bothers me about that scene. Does it disrupt the poetics of the play? Is it banal? Is it too flat? Too much of a parody? Not enough of a parody? Or, on the contrary, is it too highly emotional, too overblown? But what can I do? I've done the best I can with it.

Vlasta Have you looked at them yet?

Rieger Looked at what?

Vlasta At the documents Albín and I gave you.

Rieger Not yet.

Knobloch enters with his rake.

Knobloch Well, it's here, Dr Rieger. A courier just came and delivered the eviction notice. From today on, it says, you're living here illegally. They've assigned you a bachelor flat.

Rieger Where?

Victor enters from the coach house.

Victor In some village or other about a hundred versts from here. It's too bad you were so inflexible. You might have won some concessions from them. Now, clearly, it's too late.

Rieger We'll go and live with Vlasta.

Vlasta I'm sorry, Daddy, but Albín and I have talked this over again, and we weighed all the alternatives and in the end we decided that that would not be a good solution, either for you or for us. We'd be squeezed together like sardines, and we'd soon be getting on each other's nerves. We could give Zuzana a folding bed in the kitchen for a few days, but what would we do with Grandma? Where would we put her? In the village, you'll have peace and quiet. I'd give anything to be able to live in the country!

Grandma enters from the villa with a frying pan in her hands. Knobloch exits.

Grandma He burnt the onions. What should I do with this?

Rieger Just toss it out, Mother.

Grandma The frying pan too?

Rieger Either clean it properly, or toss it out.

Grandma Where's Irena?

Rieger She's gone.

Grandma Where to?

Rieger I have no idea.

Grandma Did Monika go with her?

Rieger Yes.

Grandma Should we wait dinner for her?

Rieger I don't know.

Grandma (*to Vlasta*) Are you and Albín staying for dinner?

Vlasta We're going to Albín's parents' place.

Grandma For dinner?

Vlasta Yes.

Grandma And where's Zuzana? She was just here a while ago.

Rieger I don't know, Mother.

Grandma Did she go dancing?

Rieger Perhaps.

Grandma Where did she put her computer?

Rieger Mother, please – no more questions.

Grandma Well, I beg your pardon. (*She looks at the frying pan.*) I'll probably have to throw this away.

Victor It's not a complete disaster.

Rieger What isn't?

Victor The interview.

Victor exits into the coach house. Knobloch enters with his rake, holding an open Keyhole *in his hand.*

Knobloch 'He had women on the brain.' That's the main headline on page one. '"He never professes his love, but he's very sensual," says his current mistress. Is he faithful to her? No one knows.'

Rieger Is that today's?

Knobloch It's the day after tomorrow's.

Rieger tears The Keyhole *away from Knobloch and looks at it. Victor enters from the coach house with another copy of the same edition. He looks at it with Grandma, who has gone to stand beside him. Vlasta and Albín huddle around Rieger and read his copy over his shoulders. A pause.*

53

Rieger What kind of nonsense is this? Did they at least print the whole of our interview?

Victor Yes, except for the political bits.

Rieger Why did you let them in here, for God's sake?

Victor Remember what Tony Blair once told you? If you don't answer their questions, they'll answer them for you.

Rieger You idiot! I can't imagine a more embarrassing way to end my political career.

Vlasta You should take a look at those documents – it's in your best interest, isn't it, Albín?

Albín nods. Rieger crumples the newspaper up and throws it at Victor. Victor leaves. Knobloch leaves after him.

Grandma Where will we go? To Vlasta's?

Vlasta But Grandma, whatever gave you that idea? You wouldn't all fit in! And Albín and I have our own lives to live; we haven't time to listen to all your questions. And where would you sleep? Who would cook for us all? Zuzana will move a boyfriend in with her, and then what? Father needs a writing desk, he'd be entertaining reporters all the time – it's simply out of the question. (*To Rieger.*) Will you look at them?

Monika rushes in.

Monika Irena tried to jump off a cliff.

Rieger What cliff? Did she actually jump?

Monika I held her back.

Rieger Thank you, Monika. You're pure gold. Please, keep a close eye on her, will you?

Monika I will.

Monika exits.

Vlasta It's true we have a large flat, but it's laid out so badly that Albín and I are always tripping over each other. And you can hear every sound, every word people say. Fortunately Albín never says very much. It's enough to make you nervous about going to the bathroom, isn't it, Albín? I just felt a drop of rain. Read it! Let's go.

Vlasta and Albín leave. Victor enters carrying a document. The wind slowly rises and a light rain begins to fall.

Victor Excuse me, Dr Rieger, but a promising offer has just come up. Would you be interested in going on some kind of personal speaking tour? You could tell entertaining anecdotes from the life of a Chancellor, sex it up here and there with spicy details about other statesmen, interspersed with hit songs. You could take Miss Irena along as your make-up person. And your entire entourage could fit into a minivan.

Rieger And who, precisely, is making me this offer?

Victor The Show and Tell Tourist Agency run by Hogg, Einhorn, Midget Brothers, Gambacci Sr and Associates.

Rieger Don't respond – at least not just yet.

Grandma So, what's going to happen?

Rieger The village is going to happen. (*To Victor.*) Can you go there tomorrow and take a look?

Victor I'm sorry, Dr Rieger, but in my opinion it would be more sensible for you to pay a visit to Vice-Prime Minister Klein as soon as possible, if he'll see you, that is. Or at least write him a letter. Otherwise he's threatening to make more trouble. One has to have both feet on the ground.

Rieger My feet *are* on the ground! Are you going to check it out tomorrow or not?

Victor I'm sorry to say I already have something lined up with one of the government agencies. It wouldn't make a very good impression if I were to cancel my first meeting.

Oswald enters.

Oswald Dinner is served.

Grandma And what will become of you, Oswald?

Oswald Me? I'm meant to be going to the Ragulins, to look after their household. I'll be something like a major-domo.

Rieger Why don't you all go to the Ragulins? And then straight to the devil!

Rieger snatches the frying pan out of Grandma's hand, hits Oswald on the head with it, then flings it away and exits energetically.

Grandma (*to Oswald*) Are you all right? Come along now, before you fall asleep.

Oswald bows and exits into the villa with Grandma. Victor exits into the coach house.

The Voice I also love an empty stage. The question is, how long can it remain empty? In my observation, nothing much happens at first: the audience is simply waiting. Next they start to become restless because they don't know what's going on. Then they begin muttering and mumbling, because they're starting to suspect that something has gone wrong and that the theatre's at a loss to explain why the play is not continuing, or why the curtain has not come down. Finally, people start leaving, or they laugh. But the main point is that an empty stage has its own special content, its own message. It is the emptiness of the world, concentrated into a few minutes. An emptiness so empty that it remains silent, even about itself.

A pause. The stage grows subtly darker, the wind rises and the rain becomes heavier. A soaking wet Rieger enters. The dye he has used to colour his hair is flowing down his cheeks in little rivulets. He is followed by Hanuš, cradling the bust of Gandhi in his arms.

Hanuš I know that this bust means a great deal to you.

Rieger Mao Tse-tung admired it greatly when he came to visit.

Hanuš I'll leave it with you. I'll take the blame for it. Let them lock me up if they want. Morally, it belongs to you.

Rieger and Hanuš exit. Grandma enters from the villa, looks around, and then calls out.

Grandma Vilem! Vilem! Where are you? We're having eggs, and fresh cherries!

Grandma exits into the villa. Rieger enters with the branch of a bush hanging round his shoulders. Hanuš enters at a different spot, carrying the bust of Gandhi in his arms.

Hanuš Are you here, sire? On such a night, even the creatures of the night tremble in fear, and the beasts of prey hide in their lairs.

Rieger I have no complaints against you, ye elements! I have not given you my kingdom. Beat against me, if that is your wish. The government is here to serve the citizen; the citizen is not here to serve the government. I am a man more sinned against than sinning. It is raining. Do you write verse?

57

Hanuš You have nothing to cover your head, sire. Here's a hovel. It will shelter you a little from the storm.

Rieger You are right, boy. Come, bring us to this hovel.

Hanuš puts the bust down, takes Rieger by the hand and leads him into the gazebo, where they both sit down.

Blow, winds, and crack your cheeks! Let the all-shaking thunder strike flat the thick rotundity of the world. Crack nature's moulds, all germains spill at once, that make ungrateful man!

Oswald enters from the villa.

Oswald Where is my lord?

Hanuš He is here. But let him be. Let quiet calm his torn senses, which otherwise could not be made whole.

Oswald Dinner is getting cold.

Hanuš So be it!

Oswald bows and enters the villa.

Rieger Put a dog in office, and see how he's obeyed. The greater thief hangs the lesser. Robes and furred gowns hide all. Plate sin with gold and the strong lance of justice hurtless breaks. Arm it in rags, a pigmy's straw does pierce it.

Hanuš There is reason in this madness.

Rieger We came crying hither. The first time that we smell the air, we wail and cry that we are come to this great stage of fools. Let us have less government!

In the following scene, various characters enter from various points, say their line, walk across the stage and exit again. Only Rieger remains on stage. The wind and the rain slowly die down.

Irena How did you sleep last night?

Grandma What paper do you work for?

Vlasta Could I have a little more cinnamon? Will you have some too, Albín?

Zuzana My regards to Monika.

Bea Yepichodov broke the billiard cue.

Rieger Less government!

Hanuš I didn't come here to eat your food or waste your time.

Oswald You have nothing on your head, my lord.

Dick I've always had a soft spot for Monikas.

Bob It was right below the Acropolis.

Victor I don't want a blanket!

Klein I'm not tired, Mother.

Knobloch We couldn't care less what you think of us.

Klein I'm not tired, Mother.

Rieger I don't want a blanket.

Irena It was right below the Acropolis.

Grandma I've always had a soft spot for Monikas.

Vlasta You have nothing on your head, my lord.

Zuzana You're so kind, Irena.

Monika I didn't come here to eat your food, or even take up much of your time.

Hanuš I like you, Albín.

Gradually, unobtrusively, all the characters have reassembled on stage: Rieger, Irena, Grandma, Vlasta, Zuzana, Monika, Bea, Albín, Hanuš, Victor, Oswald, Dick, Bob, Klein and Knobloch.

The Voice I have a word of my own for this kind of phantasmagoric or dreamlike confusion of lines or variations of lines, and some minor nonsense, taken more or less at random from previous scenes. I call it a 'hubbub', and I like to put it somewhere before the end, perhaps in the place where catharsis is supposed to occur. What is it? A prelude to some final ravelling or unravelling of the plot? A metaphor for the chaos of the world or the chaos in the mind of the main character? A pure expression of authorial mischief? A product of dramatic logic? A deliberate trick? Probably all of the above.

A rock version of the 'Ode to Joy' comes up, quietly at first. Everyone begins to sway or move to the rhythm. The music grows louder, the dancing more and more lively, until finally it becomes very wild. Then the music suddenly stops. Everyone except Rieger quietly disappears in different directions. The lights suddenly come up full on stage, and the wind and the rain suddenly stop as well.

Rieger I feel worse now than I did when I was feeling my worst.

The First and Second Constables enter.

First Constable Would you mind coming with us, Dr Rieger?

Rieger Where are you taking me?

Second Constable To the police station.

Rieger Why?

First Constable To provide us with an explanation.

Rieger I'm not going to explain anything to you.

Second Constable I'm afraid you are, sir.

Rieger Am I under arrest? With no recourse? For a twist of fate? I demand to be treated decently. Ransom will be paid!

First Constable I kiss your furry little bumblebee, my sweet piglet.

Rieger is taken aback.

The Voice Could you do that once again, please?

First Constable I kiss your furry little bumblebee, my sweet piglet.

Rieger (*cries out*) He didn't burn them. I want to see a doctor! Those damned letters! My brain begins to turn! That disgusting young Gambacci! Oh, God!

The Constables come up to Rieger, each one grabbing him by the arm. Rieger resists, refusing to go, and in the end he allows himself to be dragged off, his legs stiff and motionless. Immediately after that Albín streaks across the stage and into the villa. He is completely naked.

End of Act Four.

Act Five

The orchard outside the Rieger villa. A day later. Several large pieces of luggage are lying beside the garden furniture, among them the bust of Gandhi. The painting of Rieger from Act One is leaning against one of the suitcases, facing the audience. Rieger is sitting on one of the trunks. His hair is once more grey, perhaps even greyer than before. He is not made-up, and he looks somewhat more haggard and lethargic, especially beside his youthful and elegant appearance in the portrait. A short pause. Grandma enters from the villa with a handful of socks, which she starts stuffing into one of the suitcases.

Grandma How are you?

Rieger My trousers keep slipping down.

Grandma You've probably lost weight.

Rieger Probably.

Grandma Would you like a hot toddy?

Rieger Not today.

Oswald enters from the villa with a huge armful of damp laundry, which he starts stuffing into one of the trunks. Hanuš enters from the coach house, walks across the stage and exits into the villa.

Grandma Shouldn't I be picking some cherries for the journey?

Rieger As you wish, Mother.

Grandma Are we going to clear out the cellar as well?

Rieger I don't know.

Grandma Will they come for us first, and take the luggage later?

Rieger Yes. Probably. Certainly.

Grandma Or will they take the luggage first, and come for us later?

Rieger Probably. Possibly. I don't know.

Hanuš enters from the villa with a pile of books in his arms, all of them the same, most likely a set of encyclopaedias. He walks across the stage and exits into the coach house. Knobloch enters, carrying his rake.

Knobloch They've sold it.

Rieger Sold what?

Knobloch The villa and the orchard.

Rieger Seriously? The government sold it? Are they allowed to do that? And who bought it?

Knobloch Vice-Prime Minister Klein.

Rieger At least it's someone we know.

Knobloch exits. Vlasta enters with the naked Albín in her arms.

Vlasta He was sunning himself under the cherry trees and went stiff with the cold.

Grandma Put him next to the stove for a while.

Vlasta, carrying Albín in her arms, exits into the villa. Hanuš enters from the coach house, walks across the stage and exits into the villa. Oswald finishes stuffing the laundry into the suitcase, bows, and exits into the villa.

Rieger He already has five villas. What's he need another one for?

Grandma What did those officers want from you yesterday?

Rieger Oh, they only wanted some kind of explanation.

Grandma And were they polite?

Rieger Yes, probably. Certainly, yes, they probably were.

Irena and Monika enter. Irena is limping and Monika is supporting her.

Irena! I was so worried about you.

Irena I'm such a goose. What have I ever got from you? Why do I always forgive you for everything? Why have I not accomplished anything today? Why am I ruining my life with you, when I could have been so well off with . . . or with . . . What's his name? Or with . . .

Rieger The main thing is you weren't seriously hurt.

Hanuš enters from the villa with a pile of books in his arms. He walks across the stage and exits into the coach house. Knobloch enters with his rake and an open copy of The Keyhole *in his hands.*

Knobloch (*still walking, he reads aloud*) 'Former Chancellor's Mistress Likes Dick.' And there's a picture of the reporter with his arm around Irena's waist.

Grandma, Rieger, Irena and Monika surround Knobloch and look over his shoulders at The Keyhole. *Hanuš enters from the villa with a pile of books. He walks across the stage and exits into the coach house.*

Grandma (*to Irena*) You shouldn't have let him stand so close to you. It's your fault!

Irena Get stuffed, Granny.

Knobloch exits with The Keyhole.

Irena Did you sign anything for them?

Rieger I don't know. Probably. Certainly. I think I probably did.

Grandma And what was it?

Rieger An account of our conversation. It was quite innocent. It would have been hard to refuse.

Hanuš enters from the villa with a pile of books. He walks across the stage and exits into the coach house.

Irena Is it in your own handwriting?

Rieger Just the signature.

Irena In your own handwriting?

Rieger It was just an explanation. The document I signed merely confirmed that I had listened to what they had to say. And that's true. And what if I did sign it? I have to think of all of you. In any case, none of us knows what weapons these bumblebees still have in their arsenal.

Irena What bumblebees?

Hanuš enters from the villa with a pile of books. He walks across the stage, heading for the coach house.

Rieger Can't you give it a rest, Hanuš?

Hanuš I'd be glad to, Vilem.

Hanuš exits into the coach house with his books. Oswald enters from the villa with a case of beer. He puts it next to the suitcases.

65

Grandma Where's Yepichodov?

Oswald He's gone to play billiards at the Ragulins'.

Oswald can scarcely contain his laughter. He bows and exits into the villa. On the steps he passes Zuzana, who is wearing a backpack, carrying a laptop in one hand and a bag with various things in it in the other.

Zuzana Daddy, Gerard is inviting us all to come to his place.

Rieger Who's Gerard?

Hanuš enters from the coach house and sits on one of the suitcases.

Zuzana He's French.

Rieger French?

Zuzana He represents the firm of Smith, Brown, Stapleton, Bronstein and Stoessinger, Inc. He has a lovely house.

A horse whinnies off stage.

Rieger How do you know him?

Zuzana He's my partner. I'll give the coachman the address.

Rieger I didn't know you had a partner.

Zuzana There's a lot you don't know, Daddy.

Zuzana puts her things on the ground, takes her mobile from her pocket, punches in some numbers, puts the phone between her ear and her shoulder, picks up her things again and starts to leave.

(*Into the phone.*) Hello? . . . Yes, everything is okay . . . I'll see you soon. Bye.

Irena Bumblebees?

Zuzana exits. Offstage there is the sound of a chainsaw and a falling tree. Those present on stage listen attentively. Victor enters from the villa with a cup of tea, a bottle of rum and a small plate of biscuits. He puts everything on the table, then pours some rum into the tea.

Victor The Vice-Prime Minister has big plans for this place.

Hanuš And what has this got to do with you?

Victor He's made me his advisor. But that may not be his last word. The position of deputy has opened up. The new leadership has a rather good plan. It wants to substantially lower the tax burden and at the same time increase some government services. In many ways, it's picking up where you left off. For example, it wants to put the individual at the centre of its politics.

Rieger Is Klein going to live here?

Victor He's quite happy where he is and doesn't want to move. He wants to use this place to start up some business ventures.

A horse whinnies offstage, then a chainsaw and a falling tree can be heard. A pause. Klein slowly comes on stage.

So – I've tried to speed up work in the orchard, Mr Vice-Prime Minister.

Klein Thank you, Victor. You're a pleasure to work with. Greetings to you all. Hi, Vilem – hi, Irena.

Rieger Greetings, Patrick. So – congratulations.

Klein takes a cup of tea, sips from it and takes a bite of a biscuit.

Klein I'm so sorry you have to go and live in some village. But I couldn't put this construction work off any longer. You'll only be a hundred versts away. Have you been to look at it? Is the countryside pretty? Will there be room enough for all of you? I see the carriage is already waiting.

Rieger I'd prefer that we went to Gerard's. He's one of our family acquaintances. He's got a lovely house, right here in town.

Klein Is he the one from Smith, Brown, Stapleton, Bronstein and Stoessinger, Inc.? I'm not certain, but I have the impression that he's about to land in a spot of trouble. I hear there was some funny business to do with real estate deals, tax evasion, that sort of thing. Gambacci gave me a rundown just this morning.

Rieger Gambacci? The one charged with having sex with animals?

Klein They never proved it. Now he's Chief of Police. May I tell you something of my plans for this place?

Rieger I'm sorry, Patrick, but are you even aware that they interrogated me all night long?

Klein Gambacci's people?

Rieger Probably. Certainly. Yes, they probably were.

Klein May I share some of my plans for this place with you?

Rieger I'm sorry, Patrick, but doesn't it seem a little odd to you that they came for me just yesterday evening?

Irena And then today, all those smears appeared in *The Keyhole*?

Klein I'll ask General Gambacci about it tomorrow.

Rieger Don't tell me that . . . person – is a general!

Klein We had to give him a rank appropriate to his station, otherwise he wouldn't have the proper authority, after that business with the young heifers. May I share with you some of my plans for this place?

Victor Mr Vice-Prime Minister, I think that everyone will find it most interesting. You've worked it all out in such exquisite detail!

Klein Here, where this unprofitable orchard now stands, we are going to build a moderately large social and commercial centre. It will have three cinemas, five stores, a massage parlour, a hairdresser's, a boutique, the editorial offices of *The Keyhole*, a butcher's shop, a petrol station, a dance hall, a tattoo clinic, a cinema, an antique store, a butcher's shop, and oh, did I mention the editorial offices of *The Keyhole*? And three restaurants, including a Thai establishment. Over there, in the coach house, there will be a casino. Casinos are simply part and parcel of the times we live in, aren't they, Victor?

Victor They are, absolutely.

Klein I have the right person to look after the billiard room. His name is Yepichodov. And finally, over here, in the villa, there will be a modern erotic entertainment club. The point is to fill the entire area with life, all the time. And if, during the day, the public is preoccupied with shopping in the mall, then by evening this pretty villa will grasp the baton in the relay race of life. Of course we'll have to adapt it a little. In all this, I rely on the principle of 'less government'. Which is I why I intend to license the erotic entertainment club to a friend of mine who has no political axe whatever to grind; he's a private entrepreneur who's long had the very best credentials in this field, and he's had loads of experience in many different countries. Hundreds of young Ukrainian women owe their all to him.

Rieger Are you referring to Gambacci's uncle?

Klein (*shouting angrily*) It's nobody's business whose uncle he is!

The Voice Do you think you could do that line with a little more civility?

Klein It's nobody's business whose uncle he is.

> *A horse whinnies offstage, the sound of a chainsaw and a falling tree. A pause.*

And what will you do now? Anything in the pipeline?

Rieger You know how hard it is. I've given my whole life to politics.

Klein I might have an idea. How would you like to be an advisor to my advisor, Victor?

Rieger An advisor?

Klein Yes indeed.

Rieger To your advisor?

Klein Yes indeed.

Rieger In other words, do I want to be an advisor to the former secretary of my former secretary?

Klein Well, when all is said and done, you understand how politics works and, since you've given your whole life to it, it would be a great pity if all that experience went to waste. Perhaps if you'd been more co-operative you might be higher up the ladder today, but on the other hand, it's still better than forking manure and living in shame for the rest of your life just because of some intimate little piece of filth you wrote fifteen years ago, and which *The Keyhole* is now about to print. You must know that the Intergovernmental Historical Commission – which is chaired by young Miss Gambacci – is as leaky as a sieve. So – will you take the job?

Irena He's not taking it.

Klein As you make your bed, so you lie on it. Might I ask you, Monika, what you're doing tomorrow evening? We might go out to dinner. I know a marvellous Chinese restaurant where they say the Prince of Bahrain himself once dined. You'd be my guest – and I'd pay for everything, the food, the drink, the food.

Monika I'm sorry, Mr Vice-Prime Minister, but by tomorrow evening I'll be in Paris. Jack Lang is expecting me after eight at the Deux Magots, isn't he, Irena?

Irena I had to twist her arm, but Jack Lang isn't one to take no for an answer. He's always had a soft spot for Monikas.

Grandma Are you going with her?

Irena Do you think I could just walk away from Vilem at a time like this? What would he do without me? I'm sure he doesn't even know where the clothes pegs are. (*To Rieger.*) Bumblebees?

Klein Well, Monika, you go right ahead and have a good time in Paris. I trust your passport is in order.

Klein laughs for a long time. Offstage, the sound of a chainsaw and a tree falling.

(*To Rieger.*) So what's it going to be?

Rieger I'll have to think it over.

Irena What in heaven's name is there to think over?

Klein What in heaven's name is there to think over?

Hanuš What in heaven's name is there to think over?

Rieger That's easy enough for you to say, Hanuš. You don't have a family. We can't expect Albín to support us all, can we?

Victor They're here!

Irena (*to Grandma*) Could you look after the carriage?

Victor hurries out to meet Dick and Bob, who are just arriving. Grandma exits. Klein sits on the swing. Victor takes the plate of biscuits, goes over to Klein, gives him a little push and, at the same time, offers him the biscuits. Klein will go on eating them as long as he's swinging. Hanuš approaches Rieger.

Hanuš (*quietly*) Do you think it was wise to sign that statement?

Rieger (*quietly*) Leave me alone, you pathetic little –

Dick takes a scruffy piece of paper from his pocket and studies it. Bob takes pictures.

Hanuš (*to Dick*) That was a rotten thing you did with that interview.

Bob We had nothing to do with it. It was edited by our new art director slash manager, Mr Gambacci Jr, and our new public relations consultant, Madame Gambacci Sr.

Dick (*reading from his piece of paper*) Good afternoon, Mr Vice-Prime Minister. Our readers would like to know if the new leadership will be taking up where the former Chancellor left off.

Klein We have every intention, in the immediate future, of carrying on with everything worthwhile in the preceding period, and at the same time, ridding ourselves of everything that was bad about the preceding period. Have I made myself clear?

Victor Very nicely put.

Dick (*reading*) And what is the main thrust of your policies?

Klein The government is here to serve the citizen; the citizen is not here to serve the government. We want this country to be a secure place for free, well-educated individuals. And not only for them, but for their families as well.

Victor Bravo! Now you've really given your enemies what for, Mr Vice-Prime Minister!

Klein Didn't I now, Victor? I think I'm in grand form today. I've really set their heads spinning.

Dick examines both sides of his piece of paper. A horse whinnies offstage. Oswald enters from the villa.

Irena Have you brought all the laundry in from the orchard, Oswald?

Oswald It's in the suitcase.

Irena I hope you didn't put it away damp, did you?

Oswald No. I don't think so. Certainly not, I think.

Oswald starts arranging all the luggage into a single neat pile. Hanuš adds to it the bust of Gandhi and the portrait. Dick meanwhile has found another shabby piece of paper in another pocket. He turns to Rieger.

Dick May I ask you a question as well?

Rieger Go ahead.

Dick (*reading*) Is it true that your long-time companion, the former make-up artist, Irena, has left you and that you have a new mistress, a graduate student?

Rieger I'm sorry, but I'm not going to respond to that.

Dick (*reading*) And could you comment on why you're not going to respond?

Rieger No, I could not.

Dick (*reading*) And could you tell us why you're not going to comment on why you're not going to respond?

Rieger No, I could not.

Dick (*reading*) And could you offer an opinion as to why you won't tell us why you won't comment on why –

Monika Oh, for Christ's sake, she's already come back to him!

Irena Someone has to be here to make sure he doesn't sign anything else. (*To Rieger.*) Bumblebees?

Bob approaches Dick and whispers something in his ear. Dick nods. Offstage, the sound of a chainsaw and a falling tree. Oswald and Hanuš finish what they are doing. Hanuš sits down on one of the suitcases.

Oswald (*to Hanuš*) There was a time when they sent dried cherries by the cartload to Charkov.

Oswald takes a bottle out of the case of beer, opens it, drinks from it, and then carries it off to the gazebo and sits down in a way that makes him virtually invisible. Dick turns back to Rieger.

Dick And something else, Dr Rieger. Is it true that you're thinking of accepting a position as advisor –

Knobloch hurries up with his rake, waving a copy of The Keyhole.

Knobloch (*reading*) 'Former Chancellor refuses to leave government residence!'

Dick – of accepting a position of advisor to the advisor –

Knobloch (*reading*) 'Vice-Prime Minister Klein intends to convert the former government villa into a place for use by the general public. But its former occupant, the former Chancellor, Vilem Rieger, is complicating matters by refusing to move out.'

Dick – of accepting a position as advisor to the advisor to the advisor to the advisor to the advisor of the new Chancellor?

Klein I'm the Vice-Prime Minister, not the Chancellor. At least not yet.

Klein laughs for a long time. Oswald has fallen asleep in the gazebo. Knobloch exits, taking The Keyhole *with him. A horse whinnies offstage, followed by the sound of a chainsaw and a falling tree. A brief, tense pause ensues. Everyone looks expectantly at Rieger. Dick is making notes on his shabby piece of paper. Bob takes the occasional photo. Klein, with a push from Victor, swings gently on the swing. Rieger takes out the hat with 'I Love You' on it and ceremoniously places it on his head.*

Rieger (*to Dick*) Now look here, sir. The first thing a man must do is ask himself what he thinks the most important things in life are. In my case, there are only two possibilities. The first is that from here on in my life will feed off what went before. I will constantly reminisce about the past, returning to it over and over again, analysing it, explaining it, defending it, comparing it again and again to what exists now, in the present, persuading myself just how much better everything was back then. In other words, I could easily become completely obsessed

75

with my own footprint in history, my past achievements, my legacy, and all the little monuments I have left behind me on my way through the world.

The sound of a chainsaw and a falling tree offstage. Vlasta enters from the villa with Albín. Albín is dressed normally, but he has a beige blanket around his shoulders. Both of them stop to listen to Rieger.

But if I took this attitude, I would ultimately be reduced to an obscure figure on the margins of history, capable only of tarnishing the reputation of others, of reminding others of all the famous people I once knew, bitterly belittling everything that came after me.

A horse whinnies offstage.

And the outcome? Everyone would think I was just a vain and embittered old man who thumbed his nose at a generous offer to contribute his experience to the service of his country. That, sir, is the first choice that lies before me. But there is another as well.

Hanuš Excuse me, Vilem, but if you ever need me for anything, you know where to find me.

Rieger Thank you for everything, Hanuš, but I have the impression that it would be better, not just for me, but ultimately for yourself as well, if we were not always seen together, in each other's company, like a couple of Siamese twins.

Hanuš Well – goodbye, then.

Hanuš strokes the bust of Gandhi on the head and exits.

Rieger (*to Dick*) But there is a second choice before me: to demonstrate clearly to everyone that serving my country is of greater importance to me than my personal prestige. I have been guided by that principle, sir, all my life and I don't see why I should back away from it now just because of the trivial concern that I would, officially, hold a somewhat inferior position to the one I have held for so long.

The sound of a chainsaw and a falling tree is heard.

After all, what a man does, in real terms, for his fellow man, and what kind of real influence he has, is more important than the position or the title he holds. We are living, sir, in a democracy, and in a democracy it is quite normal and common for people to hold certain positions, and then leave them again. Am I not right about that, Patrick?

Klein Sometimes that's the way it is.

Irena Vilem –

Rieger What is it, darling?

Irena You're lying to yourself, more than you have to, and more than I can bear. I'd happily help you spread manure in the village, and eat bumble – I mean humble – pie if I thought that you had a backbone and I had a reason to respect you. I'm leaving. I'm leaving for good. You can look for the clothes pegs yourself, wrap a blanket round you yourself, make your own hot toddies. Or you can get Weissenmütelhofová to do it all for you. Come on, Monika. We're leaving.

Irena steps up to Rieger sharply and sweeps the cap with 'I Love You' on it off his head, tosses it away, grabs two large suitcases, and exits. Monika takes one suitcase and exits as well.

Rieger She'll be back. She's always come back before.

The Voice I don't know whether it's better to have Irena come back again, or to have her leave Rieger for good.

Whichever it is, it would have to happen, or at least something should tell us it will happen, within the play itself, which means now, or in the next few minutes. When the play ends, it's all over. The play's world ends when the play ends, and all that remains is our impression, our interpretation, our memories, our joy, or our boredom. But I don't want to hold things up while I make up my mind, either. So, I'll leave the matter open. I won't be the first author, nor the last, who left things open-ended, not because he intended to, but simply because he didn't know what else to do.

A horse whinnies offstage.

Rieger And something else, sir. Please be aware that the very fact that civilisation is now global has boundless consequences in the sphere of politics as well. One of them is the burgeoning influence of experts, of specialists, of people with specific knowledge, because it is increasingly difficult for a top politician to know everything or have an opinion about everything. As a result, the influence and the importance of advisors is growing every day, along with the dependence of politicians upon them.

Offstage, the sound of a chainsaw and a falling tree.

After all, who does the math when it comes to lowering taxes? Who decides how many thousands of bureaucrats have to be fired to make room for less government? Who decides how many fighter planes offered for sale by General Gambacci's aunt are needed to make this country a safe place? The advisors, that's who. And how do the advisors know with any certainty what's what? Why, they get it from their advisors! I dare say, sir, that as the advisor to an advisor, I may well have a greater influence on the realisation of my ideals than I had when I was Chancellor, which burdened me with so many purely ceremonial duties, often to the detriment of my ability to ensure that the individual was really at the centre of my politics.

A horse whinnies offstage. Bob again whispers something to Dick.

Dick Does your change of attitude toward the new leadership have anything to do with your midnight interrogation, and with some of the archival material that young Miss Gambacci's commission unearthed?

Rieger As for the interrogation, as you call it, it involved no more than providing a standard explanation. And the archival material, as you call it? They were no more than standard forgeries. But that's not important. What is important is that at this moment I wish to serve my country where my country at this moment in time most needs my help and where I can best be of service to it. Politics is service. We want well-rounded families. Long live growth! It's all about the future. Blow wind, and crack your cheeks! The world is a great stage of fools! My trousers are slipping down! Check!

Klein, with Victor's help, slows down and gradually stops the swing. Offstage is the sound of a chainsaw and a falling tree.

Albín That was one of the finest, most balanced speeches I've ever heard you give, Vilem. You overstated nothing, and understated nothing either. Am I not right, Vlasta?

Vlasta Albín, you talk too much.

Klein Albín is right. Vilem spoke like a man.

Victor That's exactly what I was about to say, Mr Vice-Prime Minister. The advisor to the advisor spoke like a man.

Klein Even though he may have slightly exaggerated the importance of being an advisor to the advisor.

Victor Yes, indeed, Mr Vice-Prime Minister. Advisors to advisors certainly don't play such an important role, at least not in our country. I would say that at this moment, and in this country, the greatest influence on politics lies with the Vice-Prime Minister.

Klein Though in the future, when all is said and done, the most influential of all ought to be the Chancellor.

Klein laughs for a long time. Grandma rushes in.

Grandma The carriage is waiting!

Grandma takes the portrait of Rieger; Dick, Vlasta and Albín each take two suitcases; and they all exit. Bob exits too, but he takes nothing with him because he is shooting the departure. Rieger throws the last piece of luggage over his shoulder.

Klein Come back and see the place when everything is finished. You always were fond of sex clubs. Remember Bangkok, fifteen years ago?

Rieger Goodbye, house. Goodbye, orchard. Goodbye, gazebo.

Rieger picks up the hat with 'I Love You' on it, puts it on, only to sweep it off again and bow ceremoniously to Klein. Then he puts the cap back on, picks up the bust of Gandhi, and exits. Knobloch, carrying his rake, rushes in and calls out to Klein.

Knobloch Wouldn't you like some of this cherry wood for your fireplace? It makes an excellent fire.

Klein You can deliver a wagonload to my villa.

Knobloch Which one?

Klein How about the one where that Frenchman used to live? The one Gambacci had deported today.

Knobloch exits. A sleepy Oswald emerges from the gazebo holding an empty beer bottle. A horse whinnies offstage, and then only the clip-clop of the departing carriage is heard.

Oswald They've gone. Forgot about me. I bet my master didn't wear his fur coat, bet he put on that light one instead. Life is over before you live it. I think I'll lie down for a minute. No strength left. He certainly left without his fur coat. Nothing left, nothing.

Oswald lies down behind a bush. Klein and Victor walk away from the swing.

The Voice One of my friends suggested I end the play right here. Just like Chekhov's *Cherry Orchard*. But I think there needs to be something more for the play to be complete. I apologise to my advisor friend.

Victor Are you warm enough, Mr Vice-Prime Minister?

Klein Not really. I think I'll put on my fur coat.

Victor exits, followed slowly by Klein. Then he sees that, not far off, Bea is standing with a book in her hand. He stops.

Are you looking for anyone in particular?

Bea You.

Klein And how can I help you?

Bea Would you be willing to sign my copy of this book of your speeches?

Klein You mean the one that just came out today?

Bea Yes. *Democracy, Freedom, the Market, and Me.*

Klein Let me have it.

Bea opens the book and hands it to Klein, who signs it for her.

You know what Molotov once told me over a cocktail? 'Patrick,' he said, 'never refuse to sign one of your books.'

Bea It's wonderful that you intend to keep the individual at the centre of your politics. Thank you.

Klein You're most welcome. Checkmate!

Bea kisses Klein shyly on the cheek. At the same time, all the other characters in the play begin to enter from all sides: Rieger, Grandma, Vlasta, Zuzana, Monika, Albín, Hanuš, Victor, Oswald – who emerges from behind the bush – Dick, Bob, Knobloch, and the First and Second Constables. All gradually come downstage and surround Klein and Bea. Bob starts to arrange them all for a group photo. Then he stands in front of them with his back to the audience and starts taking pictures.

The Voice I'd like to thank the actors for not overacting. The theatre would like to thank the audience for turning off their mobile phones. Truth and love must triumph over lies and hatred. You may turn your phones back on. Goodnight and pleasant dreams!

Bob takes his place among the other actors. They all bow. A big orchestral version of the 'Ode to Joy' comes up on the sound system and plays until the audience has left the theatre.

The End.